baking day

MARKS & SPENCER

Marks and Spencer p.l.c.
PO Box 3339
Chester CH99 9QS

shop online
www.marksandspencer.com

ISBN: 978-1-84805-035-8
Printed in China

Photography by Clive Streeter
Food styling by Angela Drake and Teresa Goldfinch
Internal design by Jane Bozzard-Hill
Cover design by Mark Cavanagh
Introduction and additional recipes by Christine France

Notes for the reader

- This book uses both metric and imperial measurements. Follow the same units of measurement throughout; do not mix metric and imperial.
- All spoon measurements are level; teaspoons are assumed to be 5 ml and tablespoons are assumed to be 15 ml.
- Unless otherwise stated, milk is assumed to be semi-skimmed and eggs are medium-size.
- Some recipes contain nuts. If you are allergic to nuts you should avoid them and any products containing nuts. Recipes using raw or very lightly cooked eggs should be avoided by infants, the elderly, pregnant women, convalescents and anyone suffering from an illness.

contents

introduction

If you remember as a child coming home to the irresistible smells of baking wafting from the kitchen, then you'll know just how rewarding baking can be. For our grandmothers, a baking day was a weekly event in almost every home, when whole batches of traditional cakes and cookies would be lovingly prepared to stock the cake and biscuit tins to feed hungry families, pack into lunchboxes or set out on pretty plates for Sunday tea.

Nowadays, many of us feel that we just don't have the time for home baking and since we can now buy a good variety of ready-made cakes and biscuits, there is no particular incentive to bake our own. But there's quite simply nothing like freshly home-baked cakes, made with love. You don't even have to spend a whole day baking to get worthwhile results – some cakes take as little as half an hour of your time. However, if you have a freezer it's often worth making a larger batch of cakes in one session as most cakes freeze successfully (without fillings or icings) and can be stored for several months.

Even if you've never baked a cake before, you'll be surprised how simple it is. All the instructions you need are given in the recipes, so if you follow the easy steps you really can't go wrong. So, why not revive the baking tradition in your home, and you'll never be short of a home-baked treat to offer visitors when they drop by!

useful equipment

OVEN

A reliable oven is essential, as temperature is critical for most recipes. You'll need to check regularly that the thermostat is accurate, so consider investing in an oven thermometer. Place it on the middle shelf and preheat the oven for 10–15 minutes before reading.

Fan ovens cook faster, so reduce cooking times by 5–10 minutes per hour or, alternatively, reduce the temperature to 10°–20°C lower than the recipe states. Check the manufacturer's handbook for specific guidelines.

SCALES

Unless you're an experienced cook, you should weigh all baking ingredients to ensure success. Choose from balance, spring or digital scales – all are efficient when correctly used. Always use the same units of measurement for all ingredients – either metric or imperial.

MEASURING SPOONS

To measure small amounts, you'll need a set of standard spoon measures. Ingredients should be smoothed level with a knife for accuracy.

MEASURING JUGS

To measure liquids, choose a heatproof glass or polythene measuring jug with clear markings. Place the jug on a flat surface at eye level to measure accurately.

BAKING TINS

It's worth investing in good-quality bakeware as it will keep its shape, conduct the heat efficiently and evenly to cake mixtures and last for years. Non-stick tins can make turning out easier, but may not be as durable as uncoated tins. Flexible silicone bakeware is a good alternative to traditional metal tins because it makes the job of removing baked goods from the tin simple and effortless, and is easy to clean.

A good selection of baking tins is handy, as it's important to use the tin stated in the recipe. These are the most useful:

- 1–2 baking trays
- Deep round and square tins, 18–23 cm/7–9 inch
- 2–3 shallow round sandwich tins, 18–20 cm/7–8 inch
- Rectangular traybake tin
- Spring-release round tin, for easy removal of delicate cakes and cheesecakes, 20–23 cm/8–9 inch
- Loaf tins, 450 g/1 lb and 900 g/2 lb
- 12-cup muffin tin
- 12-cup shallow bun tin

MIXING BOWLS

You'll need a selection of different sized mixing bowls for baking, and the easiest to start with is a set of tempered glass mixing bowls, which are tough and easy to clean. If you bake regularly, you may find that you need extra bowls, so you can add the sizes you find most useful. Melamine or polythene bowls often have pouring lips and non-slip bases that grip the worktop firmly, and they are extremely hard-wearing.

WHISKS AND MIXERS

A hand-held electric mixer saves a lot of hard work when whisking cake mixtures, so if you plan to bake regularly it's another good investment. Most have variable speeds, but can only cope with small quantities of mixture. Make sure you choose a mixer with a powerful motor that will not wear out too quickly.

Table-top mixers are good if you plan to mix large amounts, as they have more powerful motors and a greater capacity.

A food processor is able to do most creaming and blending jobs, and some have an attachment for whisking egg whites.

WIRE COOLING RACK

To cool cakes quickly and evenly, you'll need a simple wire rack to turn them out onto. For large bakes you can even buy tiered racks, but for most purposes a single rectangular rack is best. Some are available with a non-stick coating, but this is usually unnecessary.

WOODEN SPOONS

A choice of different sized wooden spoons is great for any kitchen, and it's a good idea to keep some for specific tasks, as wood can absorb and transfer flavours.

SPATULAS

Flexible polythene or rubber spatulas are useful for scraping cake mixture from mixing bowls.

PALETTE KNIFE

A palette knife makes the job of smoothing and shaping mixtures very easy, and can aid the removal of delicate cakes from tins. Choose one with a long, slightly flexible blade and comfortable handle.

SIEVE

A rustproof metal or nylon sieve is used for sifting together flours and dry ingredients, ensuring even distribution of raising agents and spices in cake mixtures.

ROLLING PIN

Wooden pins are fine for general use, but marble or glass is good for rolling out mixtures that need a cool touch.

PASTRY BRUSH

A pastry brush is used for greasing cake tins or brushing glazes onto pastry or cakes. Choose one that can be cleaned easily – some are even dishwasher-proof.

top tips for successful baking

BEFORE YOU START

- Always preheat the oven to the correct temperature, so it's ready to use when your cake is mixed. Allow at least 10 minutes for preheating.

- Grease tins lightly with a mild-flavoured oil, such as sunflower oil, or melted butter. Use a pastry brush to coat the tin quickly and evenly.

- For creamed mixtures, such as Victoria sponge cakes, line the base of the tin with non-stick baking parchment; for rich mixtures and fruit cakes, line the base and sides of the tin. For very rich fruit cakes, wrap a double thickness of brown paper around the outside of the tin for extra protection and tie with string to secure.

- If you don't have the correct-sized tin for the recipe, or prefer to use an unusual-shaped tin, just match the capacity – e.g. a 20-cm/8-inch round tin holds about the same volume of liquid as an 18-cm/7-inch square tin.

- Assemble all your ingredients and weigh everything before you start to mix.

THE PERFECT MIX

- Always sift the flour with raising agents or spices before adding to a mixture so that they are evenly distributed.

- If you run out of self-raising flour, add 2½ teaspoons of baking powder to each 225 g/8 oz of plain flour and sift together thoroughly before use.

- Most cake recipes use either butter or hard (block) margarine, which are interchangeable although butter has a much better flavour. Soft (tub) margarines and oil are good for all-in-one recipes, but less successful for creamed methods. Low-fat spreads have a high water content and give poor results in conventional recipes.

- For most recipes, fats should be used at room temperature for ease of mixing. Butter or block margarine can be softened for a few seconds in the microwave to make mixing easier.

- It's best to use eggs at room temperature for baking as they give a better volume and hold more air when whisked. If you usually store your eggs in the refrigerator, remove them about 30 minutes before you start to mix.

- To separate eggs, tap the shell against the side of a mixing bowl to crack, then break open, letting the white run out into the bowl and holding the yolk in one half of shell. Tip the yolk backwards and forwards from shell to shell to let all the white run into the bowl.

- When folding in flour, use a metal spoon, cutting through the mixture with a light, quick action to keep as much air in it as possible. Over-mixing can result in a heavy, close-textured cake.

BAKED TO PERFECTION

- Unless otherwise stated, place your cake on the centre shelf of the oven to bake. With fan ovens, the temperature should be the same throughout the oven, but follow the manufacturer's instructions for specific guidelines.

- Resist the temptation to open the oven door too often during cooking, and close it gently rather than banging it shut. It's best to try to wait until at least halfway through the cooking time before sneaking a look. A quick peep won't harm the cake, but if you open the door too often the temperature will drop and may prevent the cake from rising properly.

- To test light sponge cakes for doneness, press the top lightly with a fingertip – the cake should feel spongy to the touch, and should spring back when pressed. To check rich fruit cakes for doneness, listen closely – if the cake is still sizzling inside, it is not yet thoroughly cooked. Most large cakes will shrink slightly from the sides of the tin when they are cooked. As a final test, insert a skewer or thin knife into the centre of the cake, then lift it out. If the cake is cooked it should come out clean; if it's sticky, the mixture needs more cooking.

- Most cakes should be cooled slightly in the tin before turning out, as they shrink from the sides of the tin and become firmer, so turning out is easier.

- Use a metal cooling rack for cooling cakes to ensure that any excess steam can escape without making the cake soggy. If you don't have a cooling rack, use the rack from a grill pan or a barbecue rack.

- Always make sure your cake is completely cool before storing, as if any steam remains it can cause mould. Store cakes for short periods in a ventilated container such as a tin with a close-fitting lid. Use airtight containers or sealed polythene bags for freezing.

coffee morning cakes

victoria sponge cake

175 g/6 oz self-raising flour
1 tsp baking powder
175 g/6 oz butter, softened,
  plus extra for greasing
175 g/6 oz golden caster sugar
3 eggs
icing sugar, for dusting

FILLING
3 tbsp raspberry jam
300 ml/10 fl oz double cream,
  whipped
16 fresh strawberries, halved

PREHEAT THE OVEN to 180°C/350°F/Gas Mark 4. Grease and line the bases of two 20-cm/8-inch sandwich tins. Sift the flour and baking powder into a bowl and add the butter, sugar and eggs. Mix together, then beat well until smooth.

DIVIDE THE MIXTURE evenly between the prepared tins and smooth the surfaces. Bake in the preheated oven for 25–30 minutes, or until well risen and golden brown, and the cakes feel springy when lightly pressed.

LEAVE TO COOL in the tins for 5 minutes, then turn out and peel off the lining paper. Transfer to wire racks to cool completely. Sandwich the cakes together with the raspberry jam, whipped double cream and strawberry halves. Dust with icing sugar and serve.

SERVES 8

chocolate fudge cake

175 g/6 oz unsalted butter, softened, plus extra for greasing
175 g/6 oz golden caster sugar
3 eggs, beaten
3 tbsp golden syrup
40 g/1½ oz ground almonds
175 g/6 oz self-raising flour
pinch of salt
40 g/1½ oz cocoa powder

ICING
225 g/8 oz plain chocolate, broken into pieces
55 g/2 oz dark muscovado sugar
225 g/8 oz unsalted butter, diced
5 tbsp evaporated milk
½ tsp vanilla essence

PREHEAT THE OVEN to 180°C/350°F/Gas Mark 4. Grease and line the bases of two 20-cm/8-inch sandwich tins.

TO MAKE THE ICING, place the chocolate, muscovado sugar, butter, evaporated milk and vanilla essence in a heavy-based saucepan. Heat gently, stirring constantly, until melted. Pour into a bowl and leave to cool. Cover and chill in the refrigerator for 1 hour, or until spreadable.

FOR THE CAKE, place the butter and caster sugar in a bowl and beat together until light and fluffy. Gradually beat in the eggs. Stir in the golden syrup and ground almonds. Sift the flour, salt and cocoa powder into a separate bowl, then fold into the mixture. Add a little water, if necessary, to make a dropping consistency. Spoon the mixture into the prepared tins and bake in the preheated oven for 30–35 minutes, or until springy to the touch and a skewer inserted in the centre comes out clean.

LEAVE THE CAKES in the tins for 5 minutes, then turn out onto wire racks to cool completely. When the cakes are cold, sandwich them together with half the icing. Spread the remaining icing over the top and sides of the cake, swirling it to give a frosted appearance.

SERVES 8

coffee & walnut cake

PREHEAT THE OVEN to 180°C/350°F/Gas Mark 4. Grease and line the bases of two 20-cm/8-inch sandwich tins.

CREAM TOGETHER the butter and muscovado sugar until pale and fluffy. Gradually add the eggs, beating well after each addition. Beat in the coffee.

SIFT THE FLOUR and baking powder into the mixture, then fold in lightly and evenly with a metal spoon. Fold in the walnut pieces.

DIVIDE THE MIXTURE between the prepared cake tins and smooth level. Bake in the preheated oven for 20–25 minutes or until golden brown and springy to the touch. Turn out onto a wire rack to cool.

FOR THE FROSTING, beat together the butter, icing sugar, coffee and vanilla essence, mixing until smooth and creamy.

USE ABOUT HALF of the mixture to sandwich the cakes together, then spread the remaining frosting on top and swirl with a palette knife. Decorate with walnut halves.

SERVES 8

175 g/6 oz unsalted butter, plus extra for greasing
175 g/6 oz light muscovado sugar
3 large eggs, beaten
3 tbsp strong black coffee
175 g/6 oz self-raising flour
1½ tsp baking powder
115 g/4 oz walnut pieces
walnut halves, to decorate

FROSTING

115 g/4 oz unsalted butter
200 g/7 oz icing sugar
1 tbsp strong black coffee
½ tsp vanilla essence

sticky toffee cake

175 g/6 oz stoned dates, chopped
175 ml/6 fl oz boiling water
½ tsp bicarbonate of soda
85 g/3 oz butter, plus extra for greasing
140 g/5 oz caster sugar
1 large egg, beaten
½ tsp vanilla essence
175 g/6 oz self-raising flour

TOFFEE SAUCE

85 g/3 oz light muscovado sugar
40 g/1½ oz butter
2 tbsp single cream or milk

PREHEAT THE OVEN to 180°C/350°F/Gas Mark 4. Grease and line a 20-cm/8-inch square cake tin.

PUT THE DATES in a small pan with the boiling water and bicarbonate of soda. Heat gently for about 5 minutes, without boiling, until the dates are soft.

CREAM TOGETHER the butter and caster sugar in a bowl until light and fluffy. Beat in the egg, vanilla essence and date mixture.

FOLD IN the flour using a metal spoon, mixing evenly. Pour the mixture into the prepared cake tin. Bake in the preheated oven for 40–45 minutes, or until firm to the touch and just starting to shrink away from the sides of the tin.

FOR THE TOFFEE SAUCE, combine the muscovado sugar, butter and cream in a saucepan and heat gently until dissolved. Simmer gently, stirring, for about 2 minutes.

REMOVE THE CAKE from the oven and prick all over the surface with a skewer or fork. Pour the hot toffee sauce evenly over the surface. Leave it to cool in the tin, then cut into squares.

SERVES 9

carrot cake with cream cheese frosting

175 g/6 fl oz sunflower oil,
 plus extra for greasing
175 g/6 oz light muscovado sugar
3 eggs, beaten
175 g/6 oz grated carrots
85 g/3 oz sultanas
55 g/2 oz walnut pieces
grated rind of 1 orange
175 g/6 oz self-raising flour
1 tsp bicarbonate of soda
1 tsp ground cinnamon
½ tsp grated nutmeg
strips of orange zest, to decorate

FROSTING
200 g/7 oz full-fat soft cheese
100 g/3½ oz icing sugar
2 tsp orange juice

PREHEAT THE OVEN to 180°C/350°F/Gas Mark 4. Grease and line the base of a 23-cm/9-inch square cake tin.

IN A LARGE BOWL beat together the oil, muscovado sugar and eggs. Stir in the grated carrots, sultanas, walnuts and orange rind.

SIFT TOGETHER the flour, bicarbonate of soda, cinnamon and nutmeg then stir evenly into the carrot mixture.

SPOON THE MIXTURE into the prepared cake tin and bake in the preheated oven for 40–45 minutes, until well risen and firm to the touch.

REMOVE THE CAKE from the oven and set on a wire rack for 5 minutes. Turn the cake out to cool completely.

FOR THE FROSTING, combine soft cheese, icing sugar and orange juice in a bowl and beat until smooth. Spread over the top of the cake and swirl with a palette knife. Decorate with strips of orange zest and serve cut into squares.

SERVES 16

caribbean coconut cake

280 g/10 oz butter, softened, plus extra for greasing
175 g/6 oz golden caster sugar
3 eggs
175 g/6 oz self-raising flour
1 1/2 tsp baking powder
1/2 tsp freshly grated nutmeg
55 g/2 oz desiccated coconut
5 tbsp coconut cream
280 g/10 oz icing sugar
5 tbsp pineapple jam
toasted desiccated coconut, to decorate

PREHEAT THE OVEN to 180°C/350°F/Gas Mark 4. Grease and line the bases of two 20-cm/8-inch sandwich tins. Place 175 g/6 oz of the butter in a bowl with the caster sugar and eggs and sift in the flour, baking powder and nutmeg. Beat together until smooth, then stir in the desiccated coconut and 2 tablespoons of the coconut cream.

DIVIDE THE MIXTURE between the prepared tins and smooth the tops. Bake in the preheated oven for 25 minutes, or until golden and firm to the touch. Leave to cool in the tins for 5 minutes, then turn out onto a wire rack, peel off the lining paper and leave to cool completely.

SIFT THE ICING SUGAR into a bowl and add the remaining butter and coconut cream. Beat together until smooth. Spread the pineapple jam on one of the cakes and top with just under half of the buttercream. Place the other cake on top. Spread the remaining buttercream on top of the cake and scatter with toasted desiccated coconut.

SERVES 10

strawberry roulade

3 large eggs
125 g/4½ oz caster sugar
125 g/4½ oz plain flour
1 tbsp hot water
1 tbsp toasted flaked almonds,
  to decorate

FILLING
200 ml/7 fl oz low-fat fromage frais
1 tsp almond essence
225 g/8 oz small strawberries

PREHEAT THE OVEN to 220°C/425°F/Gas Mark 7. Line a 35 x 25-cm/14 x 10-inch Swiss roll tin with baking parchment. Place the eggs in a mixing bowl with the caster sugar. Place the bowl over a saucepan of hot, but not boiling, water and whisk until pale and thick.

REMOVE THE BOWL from the pan. Sift in the flour and fold into the egg mixture with the hot water. Pour the mixture into the prepared tin and bake in the preheated oven for about 8–10 minutes, until golden and springy to the touch.

REMOVE FROM THE TIN and transfer to a sheet of baking parchment. Peel off the lining paper and roll up the sponge tightly along with the baking parchment. Wrap in a clean tea towel and set aside to cool.

FOR THE FILLING, mix together the fromage frais and almond essence. Cover and chill in the refrigerator until required. Wash, hull and slice the strawberries.

UNROLL THE SPONGE, spread the fromage frais mixture over the sponge and sprinkle with the sliced strawberries. Roll the sponge up again (without the baking parchment this time) and transfer to a serving plate. Sprinkle with the toasted flaked almonds and serve.

SERVES 8

baked lemon cheesecake

55 g/2 oz butter, plus extra for greasing
175 g/6 oz gingernut biscuits, crushed
3 lemons
300 g/10½ oz ricotta cheese
200 g/7 oz Greek-style yogurt
4 medium eggs
1 tbsp cornflour
100 g/3½ oz caster sugar
strips of lemon zest, to decorate
icing sugar, for dusting

PREHEAT THE OVEN to 180°C/350°F/Gas Mark 4. Lightly grease a 20-cm/8-inch round springform cake tin and line the base with non-stick baking parchment.

MELT THE BUTTER and stir in the biscuit crumbs. Press into the base of the prepared cake tin. Chill until firm.

MEANWHILE, finely grate the rind and squeeze the juice from the lemons. Add the ricotta, yogurt, eggs, cornflour and caster sugar, and whisk until a smooth batter is formed.

CAREFULLY POUR the mixture into the tin. Bake in the preheated oven for 40–45 minutes, or until just firm and golden brown.

COOL THE CHEESECAKE completely in the tin, then run a knife around the edge to loosen and turn out onto a serving plate. Decorate with lemon zest and dust with icing sugar.

SERVES 6–8

plum crumble tart

PREHEAT THE OVEN to 180°C/350°F/Gas Mark 4 and preheat a baking tray.

SIFT THE FLOUR, cornflour and baking powder into a large bowl and rub in the butter with your fingertips. Stir in the nuts and sugar with just enough milk to bind together.

REMOVE about a quarter of the mixture, cover and place in the refrigerator. Gently knead together the remaining mixture and press into the base and sides of a 20-cm/8-inch round tart tin with a loose base.

FOR THE FILLING, halve, stone then quarter the plums and toss with the cornflour, sugar and orange rind. Arrange the plums over the pastry.

REMOVE THE RESERVED DOUGH from the refrigerator and, using your fingertips, crumble over the plums.

PLACE THE TART on the baking tray and bake in the preheated oven for 40–45 minutes, until lightly browned and bubbling. Serve cut into slices with crème fraîche or yogurt.

SERVES 8-10

DOUGH

175 g/6 oz plain flour
1 tbsp cornflour
½ tsp baking powder
100 g/3½ oz unsalted butter
40 g/1½ oz hazelnuts, finely chopped
40 g/1½ oz caster sugar
2–3 tbsp milk

FILLING

400 g/14 oz ripe red plums
1 tbsp cornflour
3 tbsp caster sugar
finely grated rind of 1 small orange

crème fraîche or Greek-style yogurt, to serve

pecan tart

PASTRY

200 g/7 oz plain flour, plus extra for dusting
115 g/4 oz unsalted butter
2 tbsp caster sugar
a little cold water

FILLING

70 g/2½ oz unsalted butter
100 g/3½ oz light muscovado sugar
140 g/5 oz golden syrup
2 large eggs, beaten
1 tsp vanilla essence
115 g/4 oz pecan nuts

FOR THE PASTRY, place the flour in a bowl and rub in the butter with your fingertips until it resembles fine breadcrumbs. Stir in the caster sugar and add enough cold water to mix to a firm dough. Wrap in cling film and chill for 15 minutes, until firm enough to roll out.

PREHEAT THE OVEN to 200°C/400°F/Gas Mark 6. Roll out the pastry on a lightly floured surface and use to line a 23-cm/9-inch round tart tin with a loose base. Prick the base with a fork. Chill for 15 minutes.

PLACE THE TART TIN on a baking tray and line with a sheet of baking parchment and baking beans. Bake blind in the preheated oven for 10 minutes. Remove the baking beans and parchment and bake for a further 5 minutes. Reduce the oven temperature to 180°C/350°F/Gas Mark 4.

FOR THE FILLING, place the butter, muscovado sugar and golden syrup in a pan and heat gently until melted. Remove from the heat and quickly beat in the eggs and vanilla essence.

COARSELY CHOP the pecans and stir into the mixture. Pour into the pastry case and bake for 35–40 minutes, until the filling is just set. Serve warm or cold.

SERVES 8

family favourites

apple pie

PASTRY

350 g/12 oz plain flour
pinch of salt
85 g/3 oz butter or margarine, cut into small pieces
85 g/3 oz lard or white vegetable fat, cut into small pieces
about 6 tbsp cold water
beaten egg or milk, for glazing

FILLING

750 g–1 kg/1 lb 10 oz–2 lb 4 oz cooking apples, peeled, cored and sliced
125 g/4½ oz soft light brown or caster sugar, plus extra for sprinkling
½–1 tsp ground cinnamon, mixed spice or ground ginger
about 1–2 tbsp water

TO MAKE THE PASTRY, sift the flour and salt into a mixing bowl. Add the butter and lard, and rub in with your fingertips until the mixture resembles fine breadcrumbs. Add enough cold water to mix to a firm dough. Wrap in cling film and chill in the refrigerator for 30 minutes.

PREHEAT THE OVEN to 220°C/425°F/Gas Mark 7. Roll out almost two thirds of the pastry thinly and use to line a deep 23-cm/9-inch pie plate or pie tin.

FOR THE FILLING, mix the apples with the sugar and spice, and pack into the pastry case – the filling can come up above the rim. Add the water, if needed, particularly if the apples are not very juicy.

ROLL OUT the remaining pastry to form a lid. Dampen the edges of the pie rim with water and position the lid, pressing the edges firmly together. Trim and crimp the edges.

USE THE PASTRY TRIMMINGS to cut out leaves or other shapes to decorate the top of the pie. Dampen and attach. Glaze the top of the pie with beaten egg or milk, make 1 or 2 slits in the top and place the pie on a baking sheet.

BAKE IN THE PREHEATED OVEN for 20 minutes, then reduce the temperature to 180°C/350°F/Gas Mark 4 and bake for a further 30 minutes, or until the pastry is a light golden brown. Serve hot or cold, sprinkled with sugar.

SERVES 6–8

lemon meringue pie

PASTRY

150 g/5½ oz plain flour, plus extra for dusting

85 g/3 oz butter, cut into small pieces, plus extra for greasing

35 g/1¼ oz icing sugar, sifted

finely grated rind of ½ lemon

½ egg yolk, beaten

1½ tbsp milk

FILLING

3 tbsp cornflour

300 ml/10 fl oz water

juice and grated rind of 2 lemons

175 g/6 oz caster sugar

2 eggs, separated

TO MAKE THE PASTRY, sift the flour into a bowl. Rub in the butter with your fingertips until the mixture resembles fine breadcrumbs. Mix in the remaining ingredients. Knead briefly on a lightly floured work surface. Wrap in cling film and chill in the refrigerator for 30 minutes.

PREHEAT THE OVEN to 180°C/350°F/Gas Mark 4. Grease a 20-cm/8-inch round tart tin with butter. Roll out the pastry to a thickness of 5 mm/¼ inch; use it to line the base and sides of the tin. Prick all over with a fork, line with baking parchment and fill with baking beans. Bake in the preheated oven for 15 minutes. Remove the pastry case from the oven and take out the parchment and beans. Reduce the temperature to 150°C/300°F/Gas Mark 2.

FOR THE FILLING, mix the cornflour with a little of the water to form a paste. Put the remaining water in a saucepan. Stir in the lemon juice and rind and cornflour paste. Bring to the boil, stirring. Cook for 2 minutes. Cool a little. Stir in 5 tablespoons of the caster sugar and the egg yolks, and pour into the pastry case.

WHISK THE EGG WHITES in a clean, grease-free bowl until stiff. Gradually whisk in the remaining caster sugar and spread over the pie. Bake for a further 40 minutes. Remove from the oven, cool and serve.

SERVES 6-8

double chocolate brownies

PREHEAT THE OVEN to 180°C/350°F/Gas Mark 4. Grease and line the base of a 18-cm/7-inch square cake tin. Place the butter and chocolate in a small heatproof bowl set over a saucepan of gently simmering water until melted. Stir until smooth. Leave to cool slightly. Stir in the sugar, salt and vanilla essence. Add the eggs, one at a time, and stir until blended.

SIFT THE FLOUR and cocoa powder into the mixture and beat until smooth. Stir in the chocolate chips, then pour the mixture into the prepared tin. Bake in the preheated oven for 35–40 minutes, or until the top is evenly coloured and a cocktail stick inserted into the centre comes out almost clean. Leave to cool slightly while preparing the sauce.

TO MAKE THE SAUCE, place the butter, sugar, milk, cream and golden syrup in a small saucepan and heat gently until the sugar has dissolved. Bring to the boil and stir for 10 minutes, or until the mixture is caramel-coloured. Remove from the heat and add the chocolate. Stir until smooth. Cut the brownies into squares and serve immediately with the sauce.

MAKES 9

115 g/4 oz butter, plus extra for greasing
115 g/4 oz plain chocolate, broken into pieces
300 g/10½ oz golden caster sugar
pinch of salt
1 tsp vanilla essence
2 large eggs
140 g/5 oz plain flour
2 tbsp cocoa powder
100 g/3½ oz white chocolate chips

FUDGE SAUCE

4 tbsp butter
225 g/8 oz golden caster sugar
150 ml/5 fl oz milk
250 ml/9 fl oz double cream
225 g/8 oz golden syrup
200 g/7 oz plain chocolate, broken into pieces

classic cherry cake

- 250 g/9 oz glacé cherries, quartered
- 85 g/3 oz ground almonds
- 200 g/7 oz plain flour
- 1 tsp baking powder
- 200 g/7 oz unsalted butter, plus extra for greasing
- 200 g/7 oz caster sugar
- 3 large eggs
- finely grated rind and juice of 1 lemon
- 6 sugar cubes, crushed

PREHEAT THE OVEN to 180°C/350°F/Gas Mark 4. Grease a 20-cm/8-inch round cake tin and line the base and sides with non-stick baking parchment.

STIR TOGETHER the cherries, ground almonds and 1 tablespoon of the flour. Sift the remaining flour into a separate bowl with the baking powder.

CREAM TOGETHER the butter and sugar until light in colour and fluffy in texture. Gradually add the eggs, beating hard with each addition, until evenly mixed.

ADD THE FLOUR MIXTURE and fold lightly and evenly into the creamed mixture with a metal spoon. Add the cherry mixture and fold in evenly. Finally, fold in the lemon rind and juice.

SPOON THE MIXTURE into the prepared cake tin and sprinkle with the crushed sugar cubes. Bake in the preheated oven for 1–1¼ hours or until risen, golden brown and the cake is just beginning to shrink away from the sides of the tin.

COOL IN THE TIN for about 15 minutes, then turn out to finish cooling on a wire rack.

SERVES 8

gingerbread

175 g/6 oz unsalted butter, plus extra for greasing
150 g/5½ oz dark muscovado sugar
175 g/6 oz golden syrup
finely grated rind and juice of 1 small orange
2 large eggs, beaten
225 g/8 oz self-raising flour
100 g/3½ oz plain wholemeal flour
2 tsp ground ginger
40 g/1½ oz chopped glacé ginger or stem ginger
pieces of glacé ginger or stem ginger, to decorate

PREHEAT THE OVEN to 180°C/350°F/Gas Mark 4. Grease a 23-cm/9-inch square deep cake tin and line the base with non-stick baking parchment.

PLACE THE BUTTER, sugar and golden syrup in a pan and heat gently, stirring until melted. Remove from the heat.

BEAT IN the orange rind and juice, eggs, flours and ground ginger, then beat thoroughly to mix evenly. Stir in the glacé ginger.

SPOON THE BATTER into the prepared tin and bake in the preheated oven for 40–45 minutes, or until risen and firm to the touch.

COOL IN THE TIN for about 10 minutes, then turn out and finish cooling on a wire rack. Cut into squares and decorate with glacé ginger or stem ginger.

SERVES 9

devil's food cake

PREHEAT THE OVEN to 170°C/325°F/Gas Mark 3. Grease two 20-cm/8-inch sandwich tins and line the bases with non-stick baking parchment.

BREAK UP THE CHOCOLATE and place with the milk and cocoa powder in a heatproof bowl over a pan of hot water, then heat gently, stirring until melted and smooth. Remove from the heat.

IN A LARGE BOWL beat together the butter and muscovado sugar until pale and fluffy. Beat in the egg yolks, then the soured cream and the melted chocolate mixture. Sift in the flour and bicarbonate of soda, then fold in evenly. In a separate bowl, whisk the egg whites until stiff enough to hold firm peaks. Fold into the mixture lightly and evenly.

DIVIDE THE MIXTURE between the prepared cake tins, smooth level and bake in the preheated oven for 35–40 minutes, or until risen and firm to the touch. Cool in the tins for 10 minutes, then turn out onto a wire rack.

FOR THE FROSTING, place the chocolate, cocoa powder, soured cream, golden syrup, butter and water in a pan and heat gently, until melted. Remove from the heat and sift in the icing sugar, stirring until smooth. Cool, stirring occasionally, until the mixture begins to thicken and hold its shape. Split the cakes in half horizontally with a sharp knife, to make four layers. Sandwich the cakes together with about a third of the frosting. Spread the remainder over the top and sides of the cakes, swirling with a palette knife.

SERVES 8-10

140 g/5 oz plain chocolate
100 ml/3½ fl oz milk
2 tbsp cocoa powder
140 g/5 oz unsalted butter, plus extra for greasing
140 g/5 oz light muscovado sugar
3 eggs, separated
4 tbsp soured cream or crème fraîche
200 g/7 oz plain flour
1 tsp bicarbonate of soda

FROSTING

140 g/5 oz plain chocolate
40 g/1½ oz cocoa powder
4 tbsp soured cream or crème fraîche
1 tbsp golden syrup
40 g/1½ oz unsalted butter
4 tbsp water
200 g/7 oz icing sugar

rich fruit cake

- 350 g/12 oz sultanas
- 225 g/8 oz raisins
- 115 g/4 oz ready-to-eat dried apricots, chopped
- 85 g/3 oz dates, chopped
- 4 tbsp dark rum or brandy, plus extra for flavouring (optional)
- finely grated rind and juice of 1 orange
- 225 g/8 oz unsalted butter, plus extra for greasing
- 225 g/8 oz light muscovado sugar
- 4 medium eggs
- 70 g/2½ oz chopped mixed peel
- 85 g/3 oz glacé cherries, quartered
- 25 g/1 oz chopped glacé ginger or stem ginger
- 40 g/1½ oz blanched almonds, chopped
- 200 g/7 oz plain flour
- 1 tsp ground mixed spice

PLACE THE SULTANAS, raisins, apricots and dates in a large bowl and stir in the rum, orange rind and orange juice. Cover and leave to soak for several hours or overnight.

PREHEAT THE OVEN to 150°C/300°F/Gas Mark 2. Grease and line a 20-cm/8-inch round deep cake tin.

CREAM TOGETHER the butter and sugar until light and fluffy. Gradually beat in the eggs, beating hard after each addition. Stir in the soaked fruits, mixed peel, glacé cherries, glacé ginger and blanched almonds.

SIFT THE FLOUR AND MIXED SPICE, then fold lightly and evenly into the mixture. Spoon the mixture into the prepared cake tin and level the surface, making a slight depression in the centre with the back of the spoon.

BAKE IN THE PREHEATED OVEN for 2¼–2¾ hours, or until the cake is beginning to shrink away from the sides and a skewer inserted into the centre comes out clean. Cool completely in the tin.

TURN OUT THE CAKE and remove the lining paper. Wrap with greaseproof paper and foil, and store for at least 2 months before use. To add a richer flavour, prick the cake with a skewer and spoon over a couple of tablespoons of extra rum or brandy, if using, before storing.

SERVES 16

chocolate & vanilla marbled loaf

55 g/2 oz plain chocolate
3 tbsp milk
70 g/2½ oz unsalted butter, plus extra for greasing
85 g/3 oz caster sugar
1 egg, beaten
3 tbsp soured cream
115 g/4 oz self-raising flour, plus extra for dusting
½ tsp baking powder
½ tsp vanilla essence

PREHEAT THE OVEN to 170°C/325°F/Gas Mark 3. Grease a 450-g/1-lb loaf tin and line the base with non-stick baking parchment. Dust a little flour around the inside of the tin, shaking out the excess.

BREAK UP THE CHOCOLATE, place in a small heatproof bowl with the milk and set over a pan of simmering water. Heat gently until just melted. Remove from the heat.

CREAM TOGETHER THE BUTTER and sugar until light and fluffy. Beat in the egg and soured cream. Sift the flour and baking powder over the mixture, then fold in lightly and evenly using a metal spoon.

SPOON HALF THE MIXTURE into a separate bowl and stir in the chocolate mixture. Add the vanilla essence to the plain mixture.

SPOON THE CHOCOLATE and vanilla mixtures alternately into the prepared loaf tin, swirling lightly with a knife or skewer for a marbled effect. Bake in the preheated oven for 40–45 minutes, or until well-risen and firm to the touch.

COOL IN THE TIN for 10 minutes, then turn out and finish cooling on a wire rack.

SERVES 8

banana loaf

PREHEAT THE OVEN to 180°C/350°F/Gas Mark 4. Lightly grease and line a 900-g/2-lb loaf tin.

SIFT THE FLOURS, sugar, salt and the spices into a large bowl.

IN A SEPARATE BOWL mash the bananas with the orange juice, then stir in the eggs and oil. Pour into the dry ingredients and mix well.

SPOON INTO THE PREPARED TIN and bake in the preheated oven for 1 hour. Test to see if the loaf is cooked by inserting a skewer into the centre. If it comes out clean, the loaf is done. If not, bake for a further 10 minutes and test again.

REMOVE FROM THE OVEN and leave to cool in the tin. Turn the loaf out, slice and serve.

SERVES 8

- unsalted butter, for greasing
- 125 g/4½ oz white self-raising flour
- 100 g/3½ oz light brown self-raising flour
- 150 g/5½ oz demerara sugar
- pinch of salt
- ½ tsp ground cinnamon
- ½ tsp ground nutmeg
- 2 large ripe bananas, peeled
- 175 ml/6 fl oz orange juice
- 2 eggs, beaten
- 4 tbsp rapeseed oil

date & walnut teabread

100 g/3½ oz stoned dates, chopped
½ tsp bicarbonate of soda
finely grated rind of ½ lemon
100 ml/3½ fl oz hot tea
40 g/1½ oz unsalted butter, plus extra for greasing
70 g/2½ oz light muscovado sugar
1 small egg
125 g/4½ oz self-raising flour
25 g/1 oz walnuts, chopped
walnut halves, to decorate

PREHEAT THE OVEN to 180°C/350°F/Gas Mark 4. Grease a 450-g/1-lb loaf tin and line the base with non-stick baking parchment.

PLACE THE DATES, bicarbonate of soda and lemon rind in a bowl and add the hot tea. Leave to soak for 10 minutes until softened.

CREAM TOGETHER the butter and sugar until light and fluffy, then beat in the egg. Stir in the date mixture.

FOLD IN THE FLOUR using a large metal spoon, then fold in the walnuts. Spoon the mixture into the prepared cake tin and spread evenly. Top with walnut halves.

BAKE IN THE PREHEATED OVEN for 35–40 minutes or until risen, firm and golden brown. Cool for 10 minutes in the tin, then turn out the loaf and finish cooling on a wire rack.

SERVES 8

biscuits & slices

chocolate chip cookies

- unsalted butter, for greasing
- 175 g/6 oz plain flour
- 1 tsp baking powder
- 125 g/4½ oz soft margarine
- 85 g/3 oz light muscovado sugar
- 55 g/2 oz caster sugar
- ½ tsp vanilla essence
- 1 egg
- 125 g/4½ oz plain chocolate chips

PREHEAT THE OVEN to 190°C/375°F/Gas Mark 5. Lightly grease two baking trays.

PLACE ALL OF THE INGREDIENTS in a large mixing bowl and beat until well combined.

PLACE TABLESPOONFULS of the mixture onto the prepared baking trays, spacing them well apart to allow for spreading during cooking.

BAKE IN THE PREHEATED OVEN for 10–12 minutes, or until the cookies are golden brown.

USING A PALETTE KNIFE, transfer the cookies to a wire rack to cool completely.

Makes 30

classic oatmeal biscuits

- 175 g/6 oz butter or margarine, plus extra for greasing
- 275 g/9½ oz demerara sugar
- 1 egg
- 4 tbsp water
- 1 tsp vanilla essence
- 375 g/13 oz rolled oats
- 140 g/5 oz plain flour
- 1 tsp salt
- ½ tsp bicarbonate of soda

PREHEAT THE OVEN to 350°F/180°C/Gas Mark 4 and grease a large baking tray.

CREAM THE BUTTER and sugar together in a large mixing bowl. Beat in the egg, water and vanilla essence until the mixture is smooth. In a separate bowl, mix the oats, flour, salt and bicarbonate of soda.

GRADUALLY STIR the oat mixture into the creamed mixture until thoroughly combined.

PLACE TABLESPOONFULS of the mixture onto the prepared baking tray, making sure they are well spaced. Transfer to the preheated oven and bake for 15 minutes, or until the cookies are golden brown.

REMOVE THE COOKIES from the oven and place on a wire rack to cool before serving.

MAKES 30

peanut butter cookies

PREHEAT THE OVEN to 180°C/350°F/Gas Mark 4, then grease three baking trays.

PLACE THE BUTTER and peanut butter in a bowl and beat together. Beat in the caster sugar and muscovado sugar, then gradually beat in the egg and vanilla essence.

SIFT THE FLOUR, bicarbonate of soda, baking powder and salt into the mixture, add the oats and stir until just combined.

PLACE SPOONFULS of the mixture onto the prepared baking trays, spaced well apart to allow for spreading. Flatten slightly with a fork.

BAKE IN THE PREHEATED OVEN for 12 minutes, or until lightly browned. Leave to cool on the baking trays for 2 minutes, then transfer to wire racks to cool completely.

MAKES 26

115 g/4 oz butter, softened, plus extra for greasing
115 g/4 oz crunchy peanut butter
115 g/4 oz golden caster sugar
115 g/4 oz light muscovado sugar
1 egg, beaten
½ tsp vanilla essence
85 g/3 oz plain flour
½ tsp bicarbonate of soda
½ tsp baking powder
pinch of salt
115 g/4 oz rolled oats

gingernuts

- 350 g/12 oz self-raising flour
- pinch of salt
- 200 g/7 oz caster sugar
- 1 tbsp ground ginger
- 1 tsp bicarbonate of soda
- 125 g/4½ oz butter, plus extra for greasing
- 75 g/2¾ oz golden syrup
- 1 egg, beaten
- 1 tsp grated orange rind

PREHEAT THE OVEN to 160°C/325°F/Gas Mark 3, then lightly grease several baking trays.

SIFT TOGETHER THE FLOUR, salt, sugar, ginger and bicarbonate of soda into a large mixing bowl.

HEAT THE BUTTER AND GOLDEN SYRUP together in a saucepan over a very low heat until the butter has melted. Remove the pan from the heat and leave to cool slightly, then pour it onto the dry ingredients.

ADD THE EGG AND ORANGE RIND and mix thoroughly to form a dough. Using your hands, carefully shape the dough into 30 even-size balls. Place the balls well apart on the prepared baking trays, then flatten them slightly with your fingers.

BAKE IN THE PREHEATED OVEN for 15–20 minutes, then carefully transfer the biscuits to a wire rack to cool.

makes 30

shortbread

175 g/6 oz plain flour,
plus extra for dusting
pinch of salt
55 g/2 oz caster sugar,
plus extra for sprinkling
115 g/4 oz butter, cut into small
pieces, plus extra for greasing

PREHEAT THE OVEN to 150°C/300°F/Gas Mark 2. Grease a 20-cm/8-inch fluted round tart tin.

MIX TOGETHER the flour, salt and sugar. Rub the butter into the dry ingredients. Continue to work the mixture until it forms a soft dough. Make sure you do not overwork the shortbread or it will be tough, not crumbly as it should be.

LIGHTLY PRESS the dough into the tart tin. If you don't have a fluted tin, roll out the dough on a lightly floured board, place on a baking tray and pinch the edges to form a scalloped pattern.

MARK INTO 8 PIECES with a knife. Prick all over with a fork and bake in the preheated oven for 45–50 minutes until the shortbread is firm and just coloured.

ALLOW TO COOL in the tin and sprinkle with the sugar. Cut into portions and remove to a wire rack to cool.

MAKES 8

coconut slices

PREHEAT THE OVEN to 180°C/350°F/Gas Mark 4. Grease a 23-cm/9-inch square cake tin and line the base with non-stick baking parchment.

CREAM TOGETHER the butter and caster sugar until pale and fluffy, then gradually beat in the eggs. Stir in the orange rind, orange juice and soured cream. Fold in the flour and desiccated coconut evenly using a metal spoon.

SPOON THE MIXTURE into the prepared cake tin and level the surface. Bake in the preheated oven for 35–40 minutes, or until risen and firm to the touch.

LEAVE TO COOL for 10 minutes in the tin, then turn out and finish cooling on a wire rack.

FOR THE FROSTING, lightly beat the egg white, just enough to break it up, and stir in the icing sugar and desiccated coconut, adding enough orange juice to mix to a thick paste. Spread over the top of the cake, sprinkle with toasted shredded coconut then leave to set before slicing into bars.

MAKES 10

125 g/4½ oz unsalted butter, plus extra for greasing
225 g/8 oz golden caster sugar
2 eggs, beaten
finely grated rind of 1 orange
3 tbsp orange juice
150 ml/5 fl oz soured cream
140 g/5 oz self-raising flour
85 g/3 oz desiccated coconut
toasted shredded coconut, to decorate

FROSTING

1 egg white
200 g/7 oz icing sugar
85 g/3 oz desiccated coconut
about 1 tbsp orange juice

bakewell slices

PASTRY

175 g/6 oz plain flour
125 g/4½ oz butter
25 g/1 oz caster sugar
1 egg yolk
about 1 tbsp cold water

FILLING

115 g/4 oz unsalted butter
115 g/4 oz caster sugar
115 g/4 oz ground almonds
3 eggs, beaten
½ tsp almond essence
4 tbsp raspberry jam
2 tbsp flaked almonds

FOR THE PASTRY, sift the flour into a bowl and rub in the butter with your fingertips until the mixture resembles fine breadcrumbs. Stir in the sugar, then mix the egg yolk with the water and stir in to make a firm dough, adding a little more water if necessary. Wrap in cling film and chill in the refrigerator for about 15 minutes, until firm enough to roll out.

PREHEAT THE OVEN to 200°C/400°F/Gas Mark 6. Roll out the dough and use to line a 23-cm/9-inch square tart tin or shallow cake tin. Prick the base and chill for 15 minutes.

MEANWHILE, cream together the butter and sugar until pale and fluffy, then beat in the ground almonds, eggs and almond essence.

SPREAD THE JAM over the pastry base, then top with the almond mixture, spreading evenly. Sprinkle with the flaked almonds.

BAKE IN THE PREHEATED oven for 10 minutes, then reduce the heat to 180°C/350°F/Gas Mark 4 and bake for a further 25–30 minutes, or until the filling is golden brown and firm to the touch.

COOL IN THE TIN, then cut into bars.

MAKES 12

lemon drizzle slices

2 eggs
175 g/6 oz caster sugar
150 g/5½ oz soft margarine, plus extra for greasing
finely grated rind of 1 lemon
175 g/6 oz self-raising flour
125 ml/4 fl oz milk
icing sugar, for dusting

SYRUP

140 g/5 oz icing sugar
50 ml/2 fl oz fresh lemon juice

PREHEAT THE OVEN to 180°C/350°F/Gas Mark 4. Grease an 18-cm/7-inch square cake tin and line with non-stick baking parchment.

PLACE THE EGGS, caster sugar and margarine in a mixing bowl and beat hard until smooth and fluffy. Stir in the lemon rind, then fold in the flour lightly and evenly. Stir in the milk, mixing evenly, then spoon into the prepared cake tin, smoothing level.

BAKE IN THE PREHEATED OVEN for 45–50 minutes, or until golden brown and firm to the touch. Remove from the oven and stand the tin on a wire cooling rack.

TO MAKE THE SYRUP, place the icing sugar and lemon juice in a small saucepan and heat gently, stirring until the sugar dissolves. Do not boil.

PRICK THE WARM CAKE all over with a fork, and spoon the hot syrup evenly over the top, allowing it to be absorbed.

LEAVE TO COOL COMPLETELY in the tin then turn out the cake, cut into 12 pieces and dust with a little icing sugar before serving.

MAKES 12

chocolate caramel shortbread

115 g/4 oz butter, plus extra for greasing
175 g/6 oz plain flour
55 g/2 oz golden caster sugar

FILLING AND TOPPING
175 g/6 oz butter
115 g/4 oz golden caster sugar
3 tbsp golden syrup
400 g/14 oz canned condensed milk
200 g/7 oz plain chocolate, broken into pieces

PREHEAT THE OVEN to 180°C/350°F/Gas Mark 4. Grease and line the base of a 23-cm/9-inch shallow square cake tin. Place the butter, flour and sugar in a food processor and process until it begins to bind together. Press the mixture into the tin and smooth the top. Bake in the preheated oven for 20–25 minutes, or until golden.

MEANWHILE, MAKE THE FILLING. Place the butter, sugar, golden syrup and condensed milk in a saucepan and heat gently until the sugar has melted. Bring to the boil and simmer for 6–8 minutes, stirring constantly, until the mixture becomes very thick. Pour over the shortbread base and leave to chill in the refrigerator until firm.

TO MAKE THE TOPPING, melt the chocolate and leave to cool, then spread over the caramel. Chill in the refrigerator until set. Cut the shortbread into 12 pieces with a sharp knife and serve.

makes 12

nutty flapjacks

200 g/7 oz rolled oats
115 g/4 oz chopped hazelnuts
55 g/2 oz plain flour
115 g/4 oz butter, plus
  extra for greasing
2 tbsp golden syrup
85 g/3 oz light muscovado sugar

PREHEAT THE OVEN to 180°C/350°F/Gas Mark 4. Grease a 23-cm/9-inch square cake tin. Place the rolled oats, chopped hazelnuts and flour in a large mixing bowl and stir together.

PLACE THE BUTTER, golden syrup and sugar in a saucepan over a low heat and stir until melted. Pour onto the dry ingredients and mix well. Turn the mixture into the prepared cake tin and smooth the surface with the back of a spoon.

BAKE IN THE PREHEATED OVEN for 20–25 minutes, or until golden and firm to the touch. Mark into 16 pieces and leave to cool in the tin. When completely cold, cut with a sharp knife and remove from the tin.

MAKES 16

small cakes

low-fat blueberry muffins

225 g/8 oz plain flour
1 tsp bicarbonate of soda
¼ tsp salt
1 tsp allspice
115 g/4 oz caster sugar
3 large egg whites
3 tbsp low-fat margarine
150 ml/5 fl oz thick low-fat natural yogurt or blueberry-flavoured yogurt
1 tsp vanilla essence
85 g/3 oz fresh blueberries

PREHEAT THE OVEN to 190°C/375°F/Gas Mark 5. Place 12 paper muffin cases in a muffin tin.

SIFT THE FLOUR, bicarbonate of soda, salt and half of the allspice into a large mixing bowl. Add 6 tablespoons of the caster sugar and mix together.

IN A SEPARATE BOWL, whisk the egg whites together. Add the margarine, yogurt and vanilla essence and mix together well, then stir in the fresh blueberries until thoroughly mixed. Add the fruit mixture to the dry ingredients, then gently stir until just combined. Do not overstir the mixture – it is fine for it to be a little lumpy.

DIVIDE THE MIXTURE evenly between the paper cases (they should be about two-thirds full). Mix the remaining sugar with the remaining allspice, then sprinkle the mixture over the muffins.

BAKE IN THE PREHEATED OVEN for 25 minutes, or until risen and golden. Remove the muffins from the oven and serve warm, or place them on a wire rack to cool completely.

MAKES 12

lemon & poppy seed muffins

350 g/12 oz plain flour
1 tbsp baking powder
115 g/4 oz caster sugar
2 tbsp poppy seeds
55 g/2 oz unsalted butter
1 large egg, beaten
225 ml/8 fl oz milk
finely grated rind and juice of 1 lemon

PREHEAT THE OVEN to 190°C/375°F/Gas Mark 5. Place 12 paper muffin cases in a muffin tin.

SIFT THE FLOUR and baking powder into a large bowl and stir in the sugar.

HEAT A HEAVY-BASED FRYING PAN over a medium-high heat and add the poppy seeds, then toast for about 30 seconds, shaking the pan to prevent them burning. Remove from the heat and add to the flour mixture.

MELT THE BUTTER then beat with the egg, milk, lemon rind and lemon juice. Pour into the dry mixture and stir well to mix evenly to a soft, sticky dough. Add a little more milk if the mixture is too dry.

SPOON THE MIXTURE into the muffin cases, then bake in the preheated oven for 25–30 minutes, or until risen and golden brown. Lift onto a wire rack to cool.

MAKES 12

chocolate chip muffins

- 100 g/3½ oz butter, softened
- 125 g/4½ oz caster sugar
- 100 g/3½ oz dark muscovado sugar
- 2 eggs
- 150 ml/5 fl oz soured cream
- 5 tbsp milk
- 250 g/9 oz plain flour
- 1 tsp bicarbonate of soda
- 2 tbsp cocoa powder
- 190 g/6½ oz plain chocolate chips

PREHEAT THE OVEN to 190°C/375°F/Gas Mark 5. Place 12 paper muffin cases in a muffin tin.

PUT THE BUTTER, caster sugar and muscovado sugar into a bowl and beat well. Beat in the eggs, soured cream and milk until thoroughly mixed. Sift the flour, bicarbonate of soda and cocoa powder into a separate bowl and stir into the mixture. Add the chocolate chips and mix well.

SPOON THE MIXTURE into the paper cases. Bake in the preheated oven for 25–30 minutes. Remove from the oven and leave to cool for 10 minutes. Turn out onto a wire rack and leave to cool completely.

MAKES 12

iced fairy cakes

115 g/4 oz unsalted butter
115 g/4 oz caster sugar
2 eggs, beaten
115 g/4 oz self-raising flour

ICING AND DECORATION
200 g/7 oz icing sugar
about 2 tbsp warm water
a few drops of food colouring (optional)
sugar flowers, hundreds and thousands, glacé cherries, and/or chocolate strands, to decorate

PREHEAT THE OVEN to 190°C/375°F/Gas Mark 5. Place 16 paper bun cases into a shallow bun tin.

PLACE THE BUTTER and caster sugar in a large bowl and cream together with a wooden spoon or electric mixer until pale and fluffy.

GRADUALLY ADD THE EGGS, beating well after each addition. Fold in the flour lightly and evenly using a metal spoon.

DIVIDE THE MIXTURE evenly between the bun cases and bake in the preheated oven for 15–20 minutes. Cool on a wire rack.

FOR THE ICING, sift the icing sugar into a bowl and stir in just enough water to mix to a smooth paste that is thick enough to coat the back of a wooden spoon. Stir in a few drops of food colouring, if using, then spread the icing over the fairy cakes and decorate as desired.

MAKES 16

chocolate butterfly cakes

125 g/4½ oz soft margarine
125 g/4½ oz caster sugar
150 g/5½ oz self-raising flour
2 large eggs
2 tbsp cocoa powder
25 g/1 oz plain chocolate, melted
icing sugar, for dusting

LEMON BUTTERCREAM
100 g/3½ oz unsalted butter, softened
225 g/8 oz icing sugar, sifted
grated rind of ½ lemon
1 tbsp lemon juice

PREHEAT THE OVEN to 180°C/350°F/Gas Mark 4. Place 12 paper bun cases into a shallow bun tin.

PLACE THE MARGARINE, caster sugar, flour, eggs and cocoa powder in a large bowl, and beat with an electric whisk until the mixture is just smooth. Beat in the melted chocolate.

SPOON THE MIXTURE into the paper cases, filling them three-quarters full. Bake in the preheated oven for 15 minutes, or until springy to the touch. Transfer to a wire rack and leave to cool completely.

MEANWHILE, make the lemon buttercream. Place the butter in a mixing bowl and beat until fluffy, then gradually beat in the icing sugar. Beat in the lemon rind and gradually add the lemon juice, beating well.

CUT THE TOP OFF each cake, using a serrated knife. Cut each cake top in half. Spread or pipe the buttercream icing over the cut surface of each cake and push the 2 cut pieces of cake top into the icing to form wings. Dust with icing sugar.

MAKES 12

honey & spice cakes

PREHEAT THE OVEN to 180°C/350°F/Gas Mark 4. Place paper bun cases in two 12-cup shallow bun tins.

PLACE THE BUTTER, sugar and honey in a large saucepan and heat gently, stirring, until the butter is melted. Remove the pan from the heat.

SIFT TOGETHER the flour and allspice and stir into the mixture in the saucepan, then beat in the eggs, mixing to a smooth batter.

SPOON THE BATTER into the prepared tins and place an almond on top of each one. Bake in the preheated oven for 20–25 minutes, or until well risen and golden brown. Transfer to a wire rack to cool.

MAKES 22–24

140 g/5 oz unsalted butter
100 g/3½ oz light muscovado sugar
100 g/3½ oz honey
200 g/7 oz self-raising flour
1 tsp ground allspice
2 eggs, beaten
22–24 whole blanched almonds

toffee apple cakes

2 dessert apples
1 tbsp lemon juice
250 g/9 oz plain flour
2 tsp baking powder
1½ tsp ground cinnamon
70 g/2½ oz light muscovado sugar
55 g/2 oz butter, plus extra for greasing
100 ml/3½ fl oz milk
100 ml/3½ fl oz apple juice
1 egg, beaten

TOFFEE TOPPING

2 tbsp single cream
40 g/1½ oz light muscovado sugar
15 g/½ oz unsalted butter

PREHEAT THE OVEN to 200°C/400°F/Gas Mark 6. Grease a 12-cup muffin tin (preferably non-stick).

CORE AND COARSELY GRATE one of the apples. Slice the remaining apple into 5 mm/¼ inch thick wedges and toss in the lemon juice. Sift together the flour, baking powder and cinnamon, then stir in the sugar and grated apple.

MELT THE BUTTER and mix with the milk, apple juice and egg. Stir the liquid mixture into the dry ingredients, mixing lightly until just combined.

SPOON THE MIXTURE into the prepared muffin tin. Arrange two apple slices on top of each.

BAKE IN THE PREHEATED OVEN for 20–25 minutes or until risen, firm and golden brown. Run a knife round the edge of each bun to loosen, then turn out onto a wire rack to cool.

FOR THE TOFFEE TOPPING, place all the ingredients in a small pan and heat, stirring, until the sugar is dissolved. Increase the heat and boil rapidly for 2 minutes, or until slightly thickened and syrupy. Cool slightly, then drizzle over the cakes and leave to set.

MAKES 12

scones

450 g/1 lb plain flour, plus extra for dusting
½ tsp salt
2 tsp baking powder
55 g/2 oz butter
2 tbsp caster sugar
250 ml/9 fl oz milk, plus extra for glazing
strawberry jam and clotted cream, to serve

PREHEAT THE OVEN to 220°C/425°F/Gas Mark 7.

SIFT THE FLOUR, salt and baking powder into a bowl. Rub in the butter until the mixture resembles breadcrumbs. Stir in the sugar. Make a well in the centre and pour in the milk. Stir in using a palette knife and bring together to make a soft dough.

TURN THE MIXTURE onto a floured surface and lightly flatten the dough until it is of an even thickness, about 1 cm/½ inch. Don't be heavy-handed; scones need a light touch.

CUT OUT THE SCONES using a 6-cm/2½-inch pastry cutter and place on a baking tray.

GLAZE WITH A LITTLE MILK and bake in the preheated oven for 10–12 minutes, until golden and well risen. Cool on a wire rack and serve freshly baked with strawberry jam and clotted cream.

MAKES 10-12

rock cakes

PREHEAT THE OVEN to 200°C/400°F/Gas Mark 6. Lightly grease 2 baking trays.

SIFT THE FLOUR and baking powder into a large bowl and rub in the butter using your fingertips. Stir in the muscovado sugar, mixed dried fruit and lemon rind.

BEAT THE EGG LIGHTLY with a tablespoon of the milk and stir into the flour mixture, adding a little more milk if necessary, until it starts to bind together to form a moist but firm dough.

SPOON SMALL HEAPS of the mixture onto the prepared baking trays. Sprinkle with the demerara sugar.

BAKE IN THE PREHEATED OVEN for 15–20 minutes, or until golden brown and firm. Use a palette knife to transfer the cakes onto a wire rack to cool.

MAKES 8–10

225 g/8 oz plain flour
2 tsp baking powder
115 g/4 oz unsalted butter, plus extra for greasing
85 g/3 oz light muscovado sugar
85 g/3 oz mixed dried fruit
finely grated rind of 1 lemon
1 egg
1–2 tbsp milk
2 tsp demerara sugar